Graphing the Weather

Caitie McAneney

ROSEN
COMMON CORE
READERS

Rosen Classroom™

I0792493

New York

Published in 2014 by The Rosen Publishing Group, Inc.
29 East 21st Street, New York, NY 10010

Book Design: Jon D'Rozario

Photo Credits: Cover aldegonde/Shutterstock.com; pp. 4, 6, 7, 8, 10, 11, 12, 14, 16, 18, 20, 22, 23, 24 (background) carlos castilla/Shutterstock.com; p. 5 (graph) Roland IJdema/Shutterstock.com; p. 5 (snow) Mayovskyy Andrew/Shutterstock.com; p. 5 (rain) Andrew Chin/Shutterstock.com; p. 5 (sun) Andriano/Shutterstock.com; p. 9 alphaspirit/Shutterstock.com; p. 11 (stratus) Stephen Inglis/Shutterstock.com; p. 11 (cumulus) Nick Stubbs/Shutterstock.com; p. 11 (cirrus) Mark Sayer/Shutterstock.com; p. 13 STILLFX/Shutterstock.com; p. 15 Anneka/Shutterstock.com; p. 17 Alina G/Shutterstock.com; p. 19 sonya etchison/Shutterstock.com; p. 20 Triff/Shutterstock.com; p. 21 mashe/Shutterstock.com.

ISBN: 978-1-4777-2441-5
6-pack ISBN: 978-1-4777-2443-9

Manufactured in the United States of America

CPSIA Compliance Information: Batch #CS13RC: For further information contact Rosen Publishing, New York, New York at 1-800-237-9932.

Contents

Our Weather Graph 4
Bar Graph Basics 6
Fun in the Sun! 8
What's in a Cloud? 10
Types of Clouds 11
Adding to the Graph 12
Rainy Days 14
Let It Snow! 18
A Useful Tool 22
Glossary 23
Index 24

Our Weather Graph

I've been learning about the weather in school. My city gets many different kinds of weather. Sometimes it's sunny, sometimes it's rainy, and sometimes it snows!

My teacher, Mrs. Patel, wanted my class to keep track of the weather for a month. Every day in November, we wrote down the weather in our journals. At the end of the month, we made a graph to show how many days had each type of weather.

A graph is a way to easily see and compare things, such as the different kinds of weather a city has during a month.

Bar Graph Basics

There are different kinds of graphs we could have used to show our **information**. We chose a bar graph. This kind of graph uses colored bars to compare information.

Bar graphs have one line going across the bottom and one going up the side. Each of these lines is called an axis. We used the bottom axis to show the kinds of weather. The side axis shows the number of days that had each kind of weather.

The whole graph needs a title. Each axis needs a title, too. We wrote these titles carefully on the graph.

November Weather

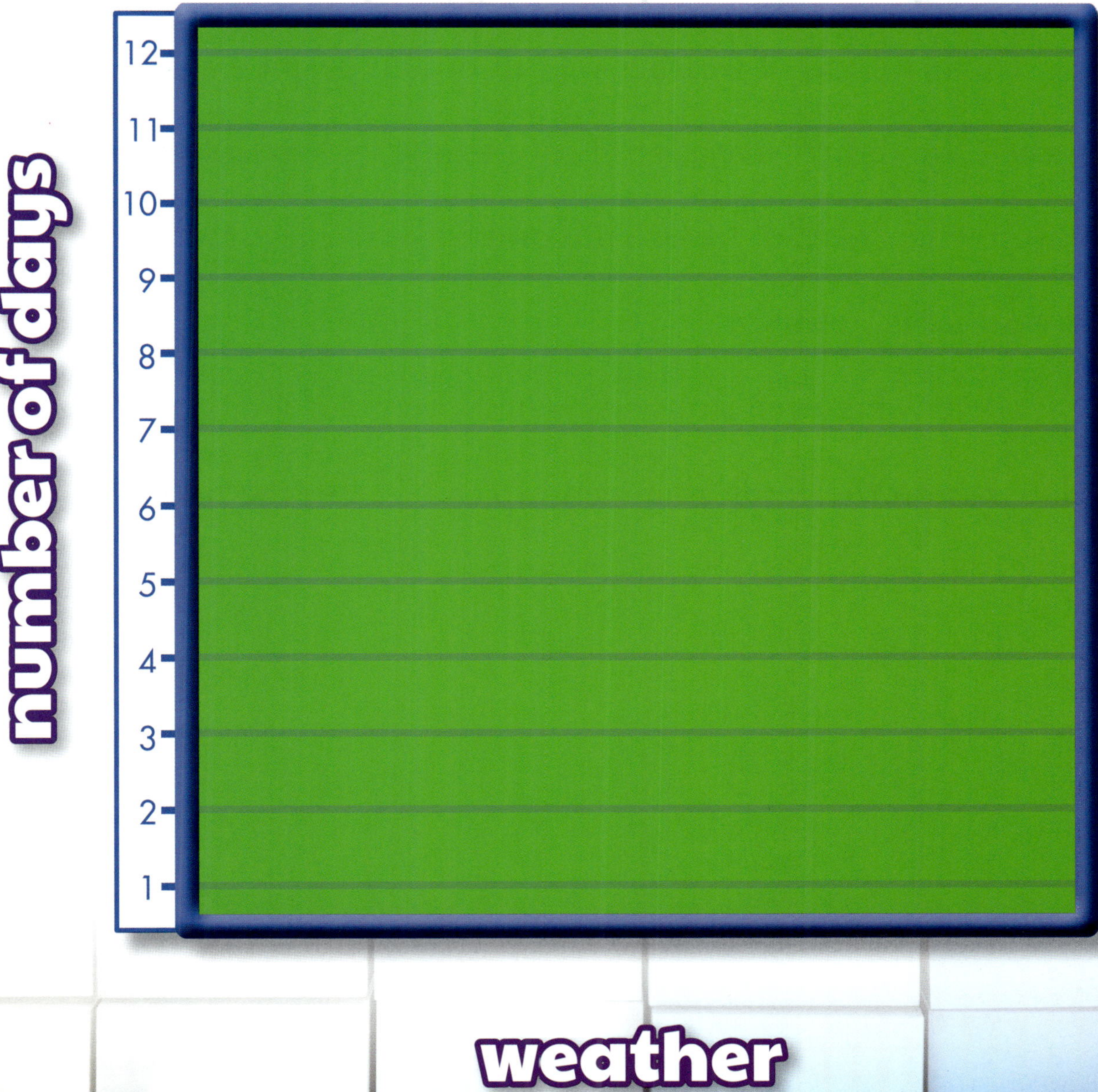

Fun in the Sun!

The first kind of weather we put on our graph was sunny weather. We didn't have a lot of sunny days in November, but it was fun when we did! My friends and I like to play outside when the weather is sunny.

There were seven sunny days in November. We drew a yellow bar on the graph that went up to "7." On the bottom axis, we labeled the bar "sunny."

November Weather

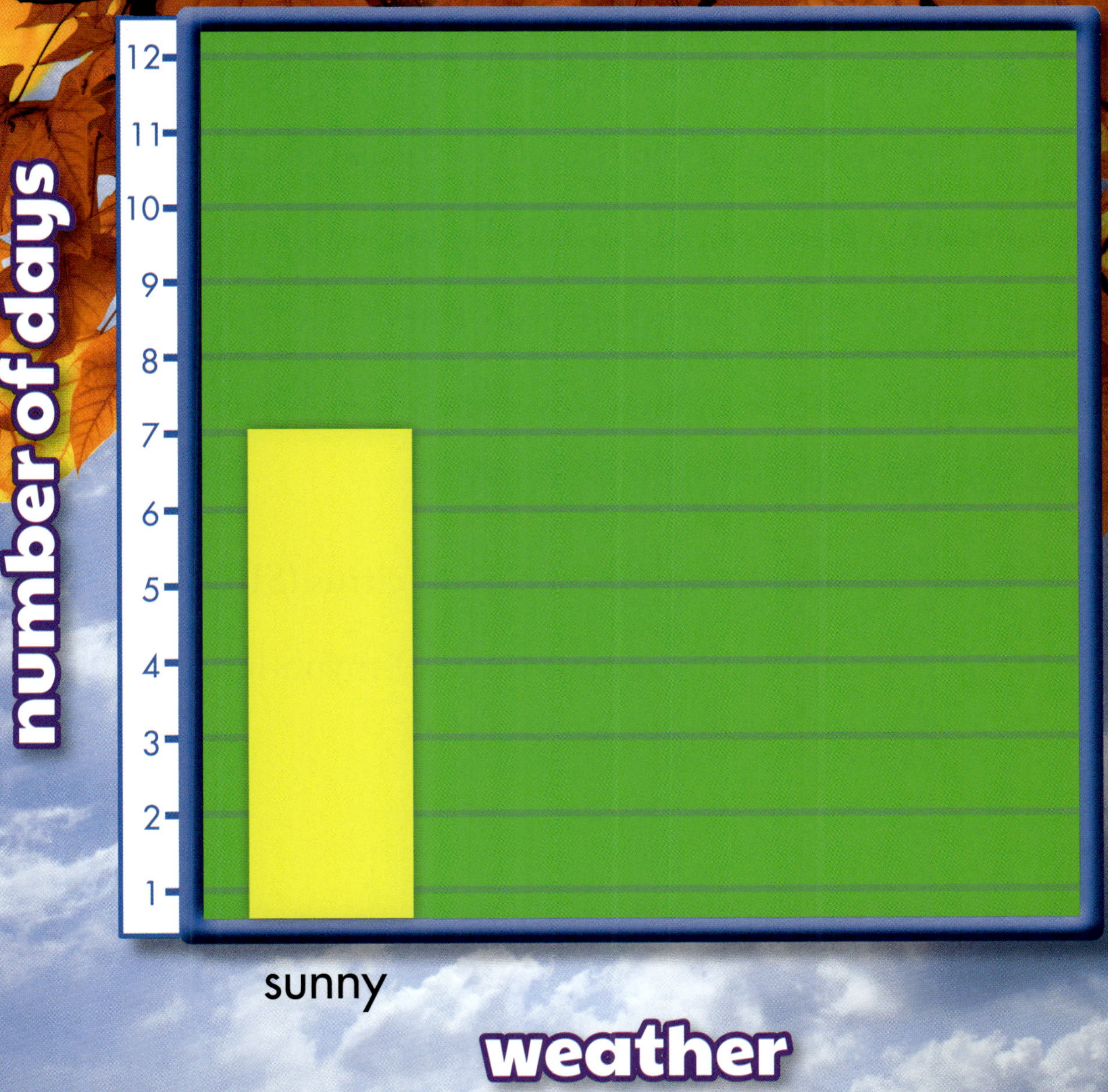

What's in a Cloud?

Some days in November were cloudy. I learned that clouds are formed from water in the air. Cloud formation happens when **invisible** water in the air, called water vapor, cools as it rises in the sky. The cooler water turns from a gas into liquid water **droplets**. When enough tiny water droplets come together, they form a cloud.

November had three types of clouds: cirrus (SIHR-uhs), stratus (STRA-tuhs), and cumulus (KYOO-myuh-luhs) clouds.

Each type of cloud looks different and can bring different weather.

Types of Clouds

cirrus clouds

- form high in the sky
- made of ice
- thin and white
- appear with fair weather
- sign that the weather is going to change

stratus clouds

- cover the whole sky
- usually gray
- can be a sign of steady rain or snow

cumulus clouds

- white and fluffy
- have a flat base and rounded towers at the top
- often appear with fair weather

Adding to the Graph

There were 10 days in November with clouds but without rain or snow. On most of these days, we saw gray stratus clouds blanketing the whole sky. On our weather graph, we made a gray bar for cloudy days. We colored the bar so it reached "10" on the side axis. Then, we labeled the bar "cloudy" on the bottom axis.

The difference between the yellow and gray bars was very noticeable!

The gray bar was clearly taller than the yellow one. We could see that there were more cloudy days than sunny ones.

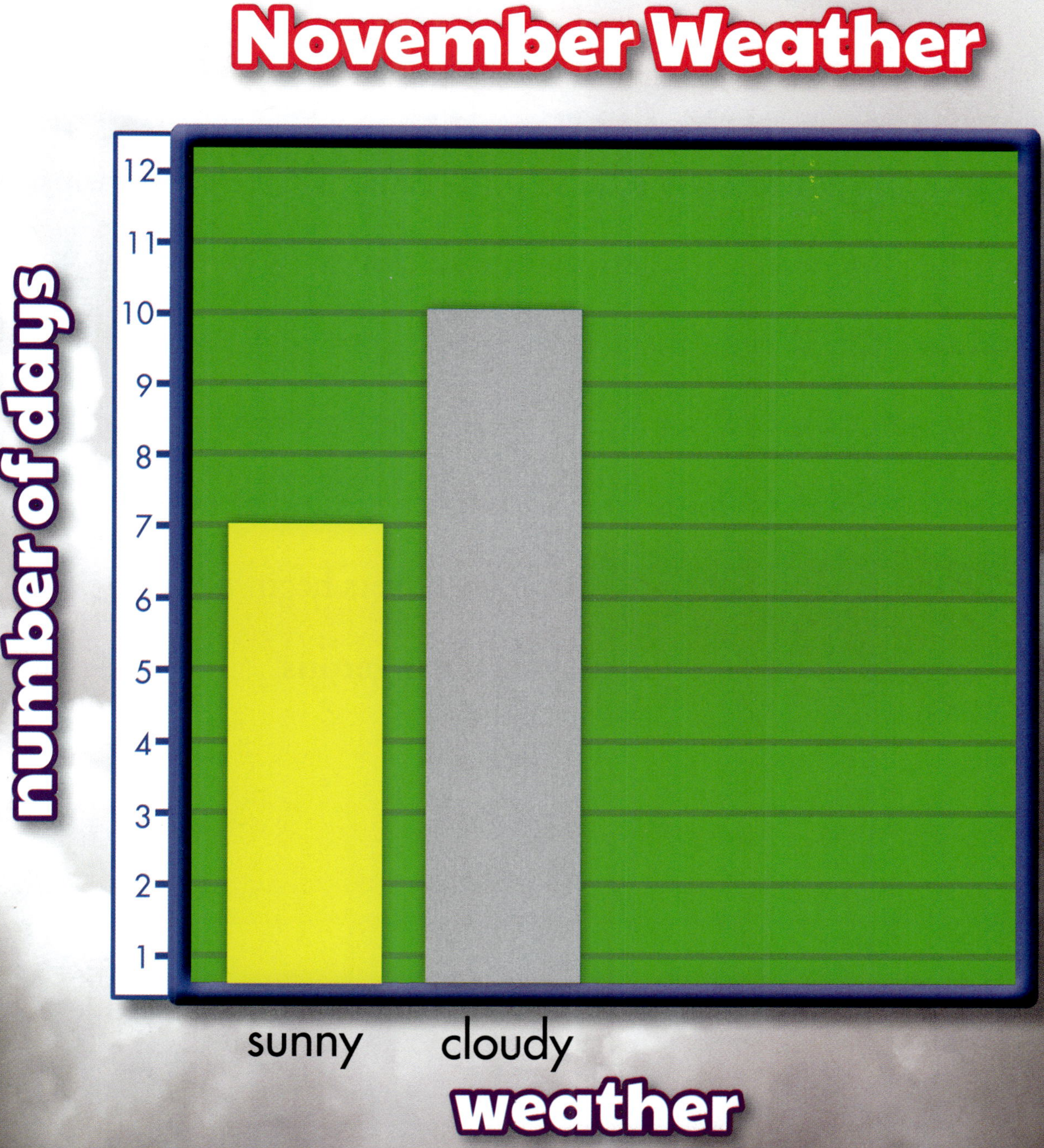
November Weather
number of days
12
11
10
9
8
7
6
5
4
3
2
1
sunny
cloudy
weather

Rainy Days

We also added rainy days to our weather graph. Rain forms from the same water droplets that make clouds. When the clouds get big enough, the water droplets start sticking together to make raindrops. When the raindrops become too heavy to stay in the cloud anymore, they fall to the ground as rain.

Sometimes it rains too much, and rivers begin to overflow. This causes a flood, and floods can be **dangerous**!

I use an umbrella to stay dry when I walk in the rain. It keeps me from being wet and uncomfortable!

Thankfully, we didn't have any floods in November! However, we did have 11 rainy days. We used a blue bar to show the rainy days on our graph. We labeled the bar "rainy" on the bottom axis. We colored the bar up to "11" on the side axis.

By looking at the three bars, we could continue our weather comparisons. We saw that November was a very rainy month!

Some of my friends like rainy days, but I don't like when the sun disappears behind rain clouds!

November Weather

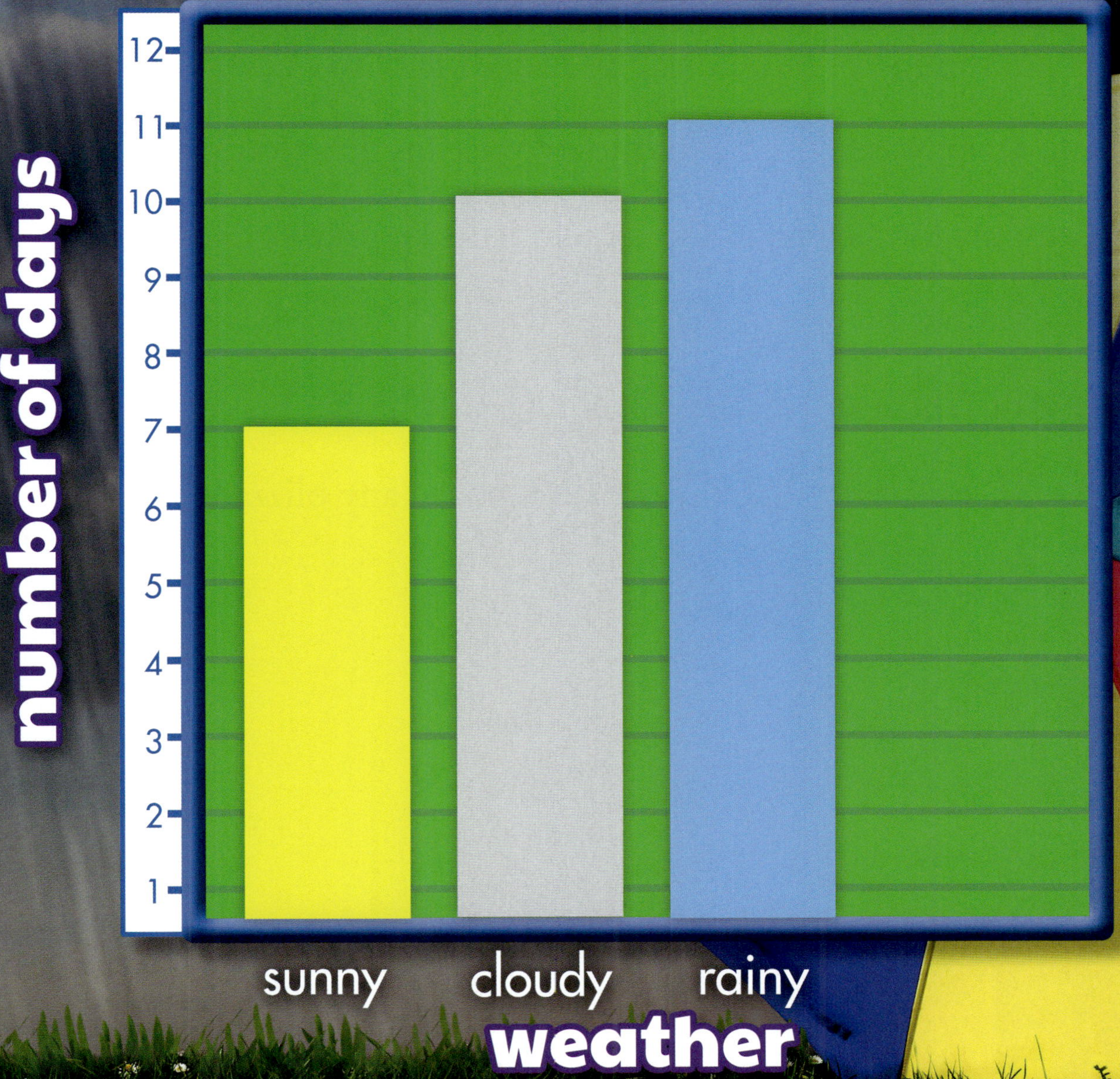

Let It Snow!

At the end of November, we had some snowy days, too. Snow forms when water vapor **solidifies** into ice inside a cloud. Snow commonly forms high in the air before falling to the ground.

Some snowstorms have high winds and very heavy snowfall. These storms are called blizzards. It can be impossible to see in a blizzard! Luckily, we didn't have any blizzards in November—only light snow.

The air has to be cold enough for snow to form. Otherwise, the water can't solidify and turn to ice.

We saw snow on November 29 and 30. On our weather graph, we showed those two days of snowfall with a white bar. We labeled it "snowy" on the bottom axis. This bar only went up to "2" on the side axis. It wasn't very tall compared to the other bars.

How many more rainy days did we have than snowy days? You can use our weather graph to find the answer!

By using our graph and your subtraction skills, you can figure out the difference between the number of rainy days and snowy ones.

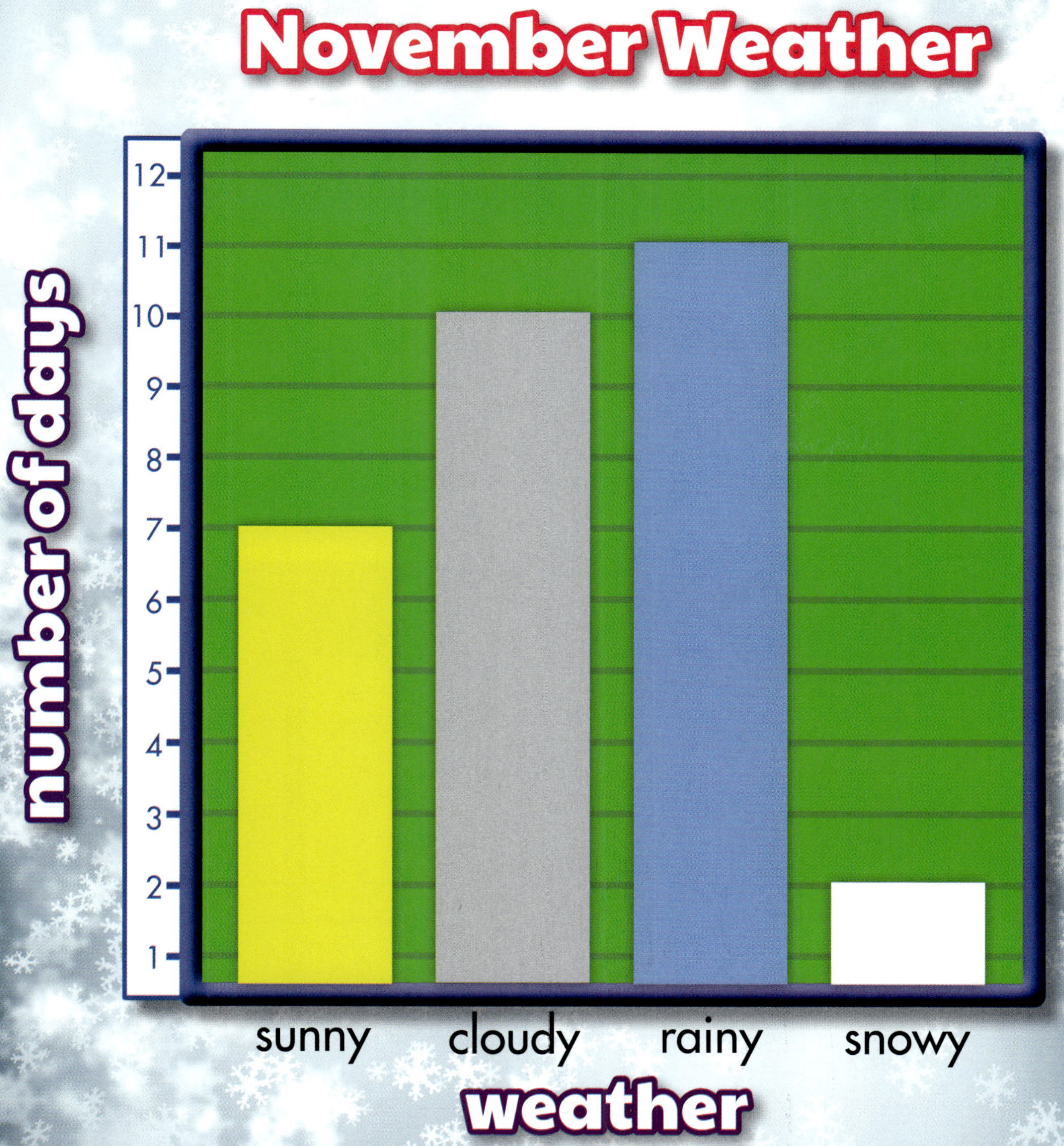
November Weather
number of days
12
11
10
9
8
7
6
5
4
3
2
1
sunny
cloudy
rainy
snowy
weather

A Useful Tool

We put our weather graph in the front of our classroom. Mrs. Patel was proud of how hard we worked on it. She asked us questions about the weather, and we used our graph to answer them. You can use our graph to answer the questions, too. It's a very useful tool!

In November, what kind of weather did we have most often in our city? What kind of weather did we see the least?

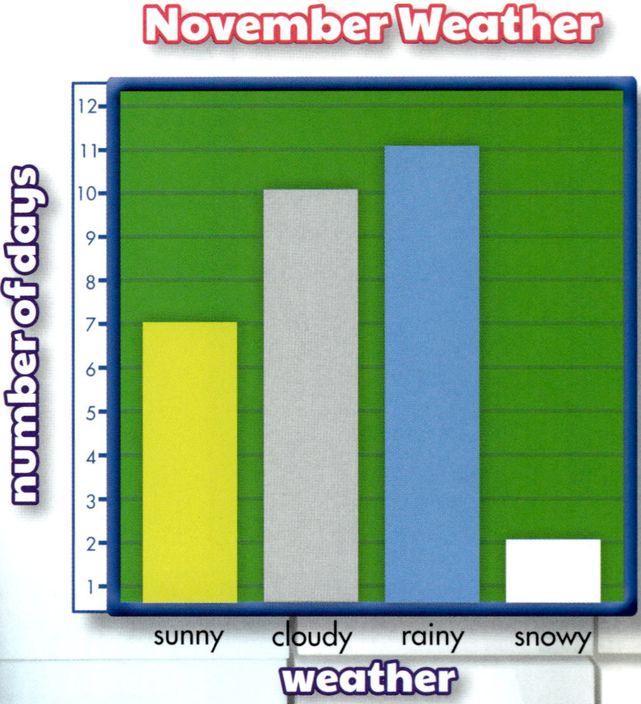

Glossary

dangerous (DAYN-juh-ruhs) Not safe.

droplet (DRAHP-luht) A tiny drop of a liquid, such as water.

information (ihn-fuhr-MAY-shun) Knowledge or facts about something.

invisible (ihn-VIH-zuh-buhl) Not able to be seen.

solidify (suh-LIH-duh-fy) To make or become solid or hard.

Index

axis, 6, 8, 12, 16, 20

bar graph, 6

blizzard(s), 18

cirrus clouds, 10, 11

cloud(s), 10, 12, 14, 16, 18

cloudy, 10, 12, 13, 17, 21

compare(d), 4, 6, 20

cumulus clouds, 10, 11

droplets, 10, 14

flood(s), 14, 16

ice, 11, 18

information, 6

rain(y), 4, 11, 12, 14, 16, 17, 20, 21

snow(s), 4, 11, 12, 18, 20

snowstorms, 18

snowy, 18, 20, 21

stratus clouds, 10, 11, 12

sunny, 4, 8, 9, 12, 13, 17, 21

water vapor, 10, 18